SOUTHWARK IN ARCHIVES

by Stephen Humphrey

London Borough of Southwark
Southwark Local Studies Library
2000

Published 2000
© London Borough of Southwark
ISBN 0 905849 28 0

British Library Cataloguing in Publication Data: A catalogue record for this book
is available from the British Library.

Author's acknowledgements

I am grateful to my colleagues - Len Reilly, Stephen Potter, Lynne Kendall and
Bob Askew - for their help with this work. I also thank Sarah Phillips for her comments
on my text. Gratitude is due, too, to the Governors of St. Olave's and St. Saviour's Grammar
School Foundation for agreeing to the use of the deed of 1347 on page 23; to Major J.M.A.
Tamplin, TD, for permitting the inclusion of the two illustrations on page 35; to the London
Borough of Lambeth Archives Department for permission to reproduce the map on page 39
and on the back cover; and to the Society of Antiquaries of London for kindly allowing the
document on page 41 to be reproduced.

S.C.H.

Contents

Foreword

This publication had its origin in a display which I used to prepare for visiting groups. The display eventually turned into an illustrated lecture, and the lecture has now been adapted as a book. Its purpose is to introduce Southwark's very interesting collection of archives, and to show how they might be useful in historical study and how they relate to records held elsewhere. The examples chosen are almost all typical of their classes, but they often have notable personal connections, which enhance their appeal.

Many visitors to the library satisfy their historical needs by consulting a book published within the past century or so. But the author of that book needed primary sources, namely documents contemporary with the subjects discussed, which allowed the correct version of events to be stated. A vast number of documents are still unused for published work; they await their researchers and their writers. The archives go into worlds which now seem strange to us - those of the parochial vestry and the workhouse, say, or even the more recent riverside wharf and the Rotherhithe shipbreaker's yard - and illuminate them in the words and the very handwriting of the people who lived in the times in question.

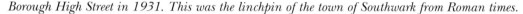

Borough High Street in 1931. This was the linchpin of the town of Southwark from Roman times.

Introduction

The Southwark Local Studies Library holds a substantial quantity of records which illustrate the history of Southwark from the 14th century until recent years. The records divide into the official and the unofficial: the one category being the archives of the present borough council and its predecessors, and the other the innumerable records of individuals and private institutions which have been deposited in local libraries since the latter were first opened in 1890.

The present London Borough of Southwark was formed in 1965 by the merger of the smaller Metropolitan Boroughs of Southwark, Bermondsey and Camberwell. In turn, the Metropolitan Boroughs had been formed in 1900 by the merger of nine civil parishes, two district boards of works, various burial boards and a number of commissions for public baths and washhouses, and for public libraries and museums. Some of the authorities which were superseded in 1900 were themselves the successors to still earlier authorities: a tenth civil parish had existed until 1896 and a large number of paving commissions and improvement commissions had operated until 1855. Of the civil parishes, the more populous ones historically were those nearer to the River Thames. There was a contrast between, say, the small parish of St. Saviour, which stood at the heart of historic Southwark, and the relatively enormous parish of St. Giles, Camberwell, which before about 1775 had no greater population than a few hamlets could muster. At the time of the first national census in 1801, Camberwell could claim two-thirds of the land area of what is now the London Borough of Southwark, but only about 6% of its then population. The majority of the official archives, therefore, derive from the north of the borough, from the old town of Southwark.

That part of Southwark came under the City of London's jurisdiction between 1327 and 1900, and after 1550 it was in theory a part of the City. As a result, there are many records of Southwark in the Corporation of London Records Office at the Guildhall. Similarly, the County of Surrey had an ancient oversight of Southwark, chiefly through its magistrates' petty sessions and quarter sessions. The present Surrey History Centre at Woking holds the county records, which contain so many references to this borough. Finally, in more recent times, the Metropolitan Board of Works (from 1856) and its successors, the London County Council (from 1889) and the Greater London Council (from 1965 to 1986), had extensive powers in Southwark. Records of these authorities' local work are kept in the London Metropolitan Archives at Clerkenwell.

In theory, the local official archives would have been inherited upon each merger by the successor authority. Thus in 1965 the London Borough of Southwark would have acquired all the archives of local government of its constituent districts since the 16th century. Indeed, those which are held in the Southwark Local Studies Library have been inherited in a direct succession from as far back as 1546. The archives, however, are incomplete; some of the former civil parishes are poorly represented. The reasons for this incompleteness are these. Firstly, in the remoter past, long before 1900, some archives were deliberately destroyed or alienated (some from the parish of St. George the Martyr were sold in 1776), and from time to time some items were destroyed by fire or flood (the offices of the St. Saviour's District Board of Works, for example, were flooded in the 19th century). Secondly, there was no real distinction between civil and ecclesiastical parishes (that is, between local and Church government) until the 19th century, and so some records of civil functions, which were kept in churches, have passed to the London Metropolitan Archives by virtue of its being the place of deposit for ecclesiastical records from Southwark. (For the same reason, however, a few ecclesiastical items have ended up among the library's civil records.) Thirdly, the Poor Law Amendment Act of 1834 took away the administration of the Poor Law from the civil parishes, whose most important function it had been, and placed it in the hands of Boards of Guardians. These boards were superseded by the London County Council in 1930. Inevitably, some of the parishes' records from before 1834 found their way in or soon after 1930 into the hands of the London County Council and so into what has become the London Metropolitan Archives. Finally, most of the older records of St. Saviour's Parish, Southwark, which might have been expected to pass to the Metropolitan Borough of Southwark in 1900, were retained by a body known as the Corporation of Wardens, which had been involved in the running of St. Saviour's from 1540; these records also passed to the London Metropolitan Archives as a result of the compilation of Volume XXII of *The Survey of London* just after the Second World War. Substantial though the archives in the library are, therefore, it must be remembered that many more local authority records from Southwark survive in other hands.

From the mid-16th century until the late 19th century all the official archives were kept by the clerks to the vestries, boards of works, burial boards, commissions of libraries and baths, etc., in their several offices, the equivalent of today's town halls. Transfers of archives to their familiar modern custody in libraries chiefly took place well into the 20th century and initially involved the main reference libraries of the three Metropolitan Boroughs. Only in 1967, when the Southwark Room was opened in Newington District Library, was there a separate library for archives and local history in Southwark. This became the Southwark Local Studies Library, at 211 Borough High Street, in 1978.

The official archives consist mainly of these categories: the vestry minutes - the equivalent of today's Council minutes - and various series of committee minutes; rate books (which constitute the single most numerous type of archives; in the case of St. George's Parish, rate books survive for each quarter-year over a long period); Poor Law records, which are most substantial for the late 18th and early 19th centuries, especially for the parishes of St. George the Martyr, Southwark, and St. Mary, Newington; records of the upkeep of roads and pavements; records of public works in the second half of the 19th century; and, in the 20th century, records of public health in the Metropolitan Borough of Southwark and of libraries and drainage in all the boroughs.

As soon as local public libraries existed, from 1890 onwards, they began to receive donations of manuscripts from private institutions and individuals. At a later date, some small-scale purchases of similar material began to be made. Over the years, these acquisitions grew into the very substantial collection of unofficial records which the library holds today and which is illustrated here. Property deeds comprise the overwhelming majority of unofficial records which have been deposited, and most of those have come from solicitors through the British Records Association. In some cases deposits of deeds have given a detailed

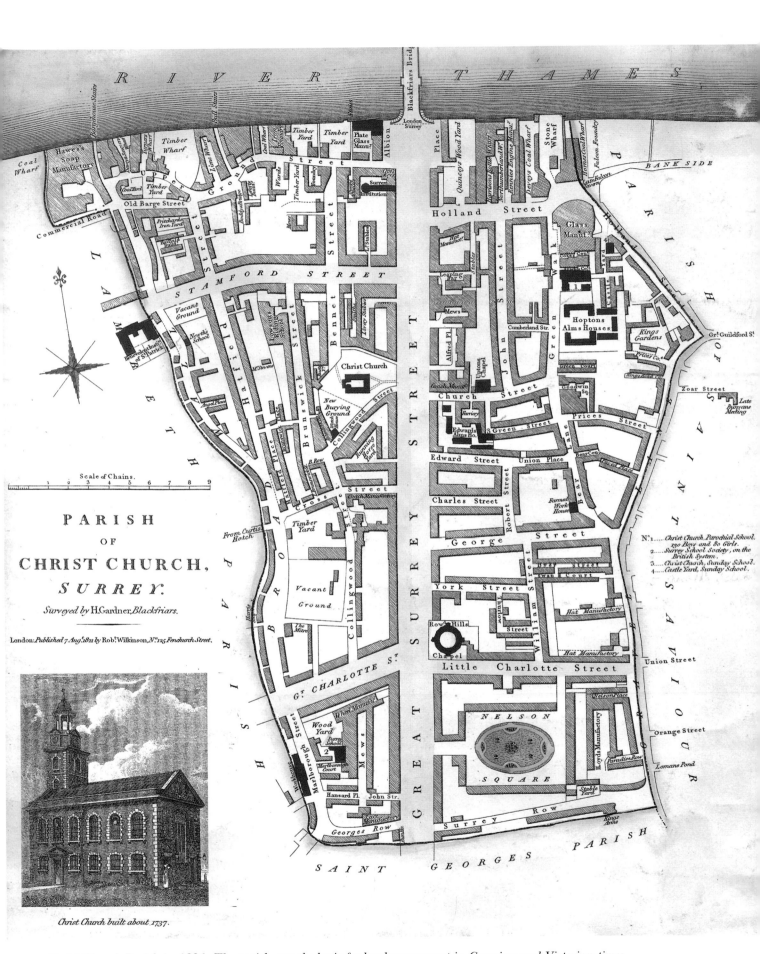

Christ Church Parish in 1821. The parish was the basis for local government in Georgian and Victorian times.

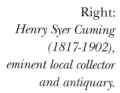

picture of sizeable estates in the borough. A major unofficial accession was the Cuming Bequest to the Metropolitan Borough of Southwark in 1902. Richard Cuming (1777-1870) and his son, Henry Syer Cuming (1817-1902), collected relentlessly from the late 18th century on a wide range of local subjects (to say nothing of world-wide ones). Another significant series of deposits, received in the 1970s and 1980s, comprised almost all the surviving records of Methodist churches in the borough, including those from such important institutions as the Bermondsey Settlement and Clubland Church.

It must be remembered that the collection of unofficial records is, in the end, a completely random one. It consists simply of those records which have survived in private hands and which their owners have decided to place in this particular repository. More such records survive in other collections, but a great many will have perished. This is especially true of business records. Countless thousands of businesses have existed in the borough over the centuries, but only a couple of dozen are represented in the library, and then only in fragmentary form in most cases. The trade of the hop merchants in and around Borough High Street is perhaps the only line of business which has anything approaching a fair representation in this collection. Entire industries - leather tanning, brewing, engineering, printing - are almost unrepresented, and the great trade of the riverside wharves appears merely in the form of a few bundles of deeds from scattered sites, plus the somewhat larger group of records from Butler's Wharf near Tower Bridge. In other fields, it might be remarked that only one of the borough's various territorial regiments (the 24th London Regiment) is represented and likewise only one of the units of volunteers against Napoleon; schools are represented by few records from charity and church schools; and hospitals, railways, the Surrey Docks and Canal, and courts and prisons are all more or less excluded from the library's holdings. Some discussion of significant batches of records which relate to Southwark and are held elsewhere is given towards the end of this book.

Official archives

Vestry minutes

The vestry was the governing body of a parish between the 16th and the 19th centuries. It was a combination of a parochial church council and a modern district or borough council. The oversight of the parish church and matters such as schools and charities constituted the ecclesiastical duties, in addition to which the ancient parishes of England were given civil responsibilities by Tudor and later governments, chiefly in the running of the Poor Law and in the upkeep of highways. For some three centuries this mixture of the civil and the ecclesiastical was characteristic of local administration. The vestry had powers which derived variously from parliamentary statutes and canons of the Church. The officers elected by its members included churchwardens, sextons and organists on the one hand, and overseers of the poor, surveyors of the highways and masters of the workhouse on the other. The Poor Law loomed large, as in the world of *Oliver Twist:* beadles, workhouses and parish relief were to the forefront of parochial concerns.

The vestry met as frequently as business required. In early times, the minutes might record little but annual meetings for the election of officers, which were traditionally held just after Easter. By the early 19th century, however, a monthly meeting was normal in Southwark's parishes. Populous London parishes naturally generated more business than rural ones, and meetings would also be held more regularly if a major issue had arisen, such as the rebuilding of the church or the building of a workhouse or a school. The meeting-place was often the church itself, but public houses, schools and workhouses were also used. In the mid-19th century, as the civil was separated from the ecclesiastical, the vestry became legally bound to meet in a place other than the church. Vestry halls then became common. The municipal offices on the corner of Walworth Road and Wansey Street were built as the vestry hall of the parish of St. Mary, Newington, in 1864-5. In London, an Act of Parliament which was passed in 1855, the Metropolis Local Management Act, reconstituted vestries from January 1st, 1856, along lines which were much closer to modern secular councils. Only the chairing of meetings by the Rector or Vicar looked back to earlier times, plus of course the names of the parishes.

The Southwark Local Studies Library holds runs of vestry minutes from ten parishes. There are 213 volumes in total (excluding volumes of minutes for specific purposes). Of these, 189 volumes derive from just five parishes. The other five were not recognized authorities under the Act of 1855 - their parishes came under district boards of works for the Act's purposes - and so in their cases there are none of the detailed volumes from the later 19th century. It was normal for seven or eight volumes to accumulate over two or three centuries until 1855, and then to have forty or more completed between 1856 and 1900. All vestries came to an end in London in 1900, when the metropolitan boroughs were set up. 'The parish' then ceased to be a unit of local government in London except in certain formal senses which may be ignored, but it survived in rural areas, and secular parish councils still exist in country villages.

Until the mid-19th century, a new ecclesiastical parish could not be created without creating a new civil one, too; in other words, to build a new parish church entailed the creation of a new borough council as well. The parishes which have surviving vestry minutes, therefore, are the ancient parishes inherited from the Middle Ages, plus a small number of new ones created by Act of Parliament or other authority in the 17th and 18th centuries. The number and boundaries of such civil parishes were more or less set fast from about 1750. The huge number of new Victorian parishes is therefore excluded from the subject of civil vestries.

A list of Vestry Minutes held at Southwark Local Studies Library can be found at the back of this book.

Foundation of St. Olave's School, 1560

In this paragraph, St. Olave's Vestry in 1560 decides to set up a 'fre skolle', later to be known as St. Olave's Grammar School. At the end of the 19th century, it merged with the equally old school of the neighbouring St. Saviour's Parish, and the joint foundation continues to this day. The boys' school is now situated at Orpington in Kent but the girls' school remains in Southwark, in New Kent Road. *(Top left)*

Rotherhithe Vestry in 1697

A populous, town-centre vestry such as that of St. Olave would have considerable parish property to administer, and much business to transact. There would be frequent meetings and copious minutes of the vestry's decisions. In less populous parishes, however, it could sometimes be the case that very little happened in the vestry from one year to another. In extreme cases, all you would find are the minutes of annual meetings. These meetings were always held just after Easter, and their business was to elect the parochial officers for the ensuing year. In this case, the vestry minutes for the parish of St. Mary, Rotherhithe, in 1697, show a Mr. Buggins taking his turn as churchwarden and a Mr. Pew being elected as a sidesman. *(Top right)*

St. George's Vestry Meeting, 1828

Notice of a vestry meeting in the parish of St. George the Martyr, Southwark, 1828 (right). Parochial vestries of the time often had business to transact in respect of almshouses and schools. In this case, nominations were made regularly to the Drapers' Almshouses in what is now Glasshill Street. The buildings still stand but are not used as almshouses. The Vestry Clerk, Archibald Campbell Russell, had a house in Lant Street on the corner of Sanctuary Street, in which the 12-year-old Charles Dickens lodged in 1824. Dickens went there because his father was a prisoner for debt in the nearby Marshalsea Prison. Russell, appropriately, was an agent for the Insolvent Debtors' Court.

St. George the Martyr,
SOUTHWARK,
FRIDAY, 11th January, 1828.

Notice is hereby given, that a PUBLIC VESTRY will be holden in the Vestry Room of this Parish, on WEDNESDAY next, the 16th inst. at Eleven (for Twelve) o'Clock in the Forenoon precisely, to elect for presentation to the Worshipful the Company of Drapers, an aged Poor Widow, who, or whose deceased Husband, has been a Householder in this Parish, and who now belongs thereto, is an Inhabitant thereof, and is a proper Person to be placed in the Alms Houses in Hill Street.

A. C. RUSSELL,
Vestry Clerk, Lant Street.

W. Barnes, Printer, Southwark.

Committees

It is an archival pattern for all administrations to create few types of record in their early history - perhaps only one - and then to divide their business gradually between an increasing number of record series.
A mediaeval bishop's register, for example, will contain categories of business which were later recorded in separate volumes. A parochial vestry similarly divided its business by setting up committees. In the 18th century, the local workhouse would often be made the responsibility of a committee. In Victorian times, numerous committees were set up. They might be permanent, such as a General Purposes Committee or a Public Health Committee, or they might be devoted to a specific task, such as St. Mary Magdalen, Bermondsey's **Special Sanitary Committee for the Prevention of Cholera**, which existed during the epidemic of 1866. The committee with the oddest title was St. Giles, Camberwell's **Slop and Dust Committee** of 1881-2, which published a booklet on its work, entitled *Slopping and Dusting*, in 1881. In the 20th century, the Metropolitan Borough of Bermondsey set up a **Beautification Committee,** to plant trees and introduce further civic amenities such as parks and playgrounds.

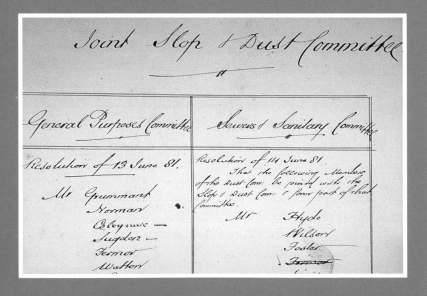

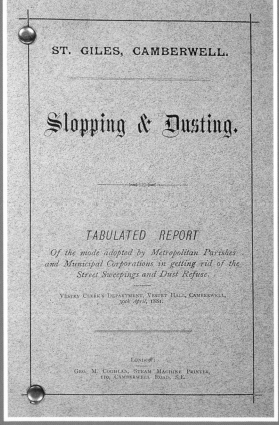

Churchwardens' Accounts

Churchwardens' accounts form the earliest surviving category among parish records, sometimes stretching back to the 14th century and so preceding parish registers and vestry minutes by two centuries. It must be said at once that mediaeval churchwardens' accounts are still infrequent, but enough exist to form a substantial subject of study, whereas other parochial series will not begin until the mid-16th century at the earliest. The office of churchwarden seems to have existed widely by the 13th century, and there is some evidence for it in the 12th century. Just as mediaeval priests were given all manner of titles (other than rector and vicar) in documents, so churchwardens of the time also appear under other titles, most famously as 'the church reeve' in Chaucer. The mediaeval churchwarden is conventionally depicted from one of two different angles: firstly, as the priest's lay assistant in the running of the church; and secondly, as a representative of the lay congregation in its dealings with the clergy. The reality involved both angles. It must be remembered that mediaeval parish churches usually had more than one priest. There were deacons and sub-deacons and priests who marked *obits* (anniversaries of deaths) and ran chantries (endowments to say masses). The rector or vicar (if resident) would therefore have had more helpers than just a churchwarden. The idea of a warden as a representative of the laity has something to commend it, for there was a division of responsibility between laity and clergy in the church building: the laity conventionally dealt with the nave and the clergy with the chancel. In general, however, it is wrong to see a sharp division.

The churchwarden came to have a major role in the care of the fabric and fittings of a church, which usually grew larger and richer as the Middle Ages advanced. In particular, he was the keeper of the church plate, which was often lavish before the Reformation. Vestments and service books were also important parochial possessions. Pre-Reformation churchwardens' accounts are almost entirely ecclesiastical in content, unlike their Stuart, Georgian and Victorian successors. They will give income from collections and fees and a surprisingly wide range of money-raising activities, and list expenditure on the upkeep of fittings and on items needed for services. In the 16th century, subsequent to the Reformation, parochial charities, schools and property begin to appear. Most of the ancient charities which exist today originated in Elizabethan times, and to begin with they were administered by the churchwardens; later, each charity tended to have its own trustees.

Parishes have conventionally had two wardens, and most people suppose one was chosen by the priest and the other by the congregation. Originally, however, both were chosen jointly by the priest and people, with separate choices made only in the case of disagreement. If parochial business was substantial, more than two wardens were chosen. Kendal in Westmoreland had no fewer than twelve. Sometimes the individual wardens had distinctive titles, which referred to particular responsibilities, usually for charities or parish property other than the church itself.

Mediaeval churchwardens' accounts survive (in the London Metropolitan Archives) for just one parish in Southwark, that of

St. Margaret, which was merged in 1540 with that of St. Mary Magdalen Overy to form the new parish of St. Saviour. The new parish church was the former Augustinian Priory Church of St. Mary Overy. In 1905 it was to become Southwark Cathedral. The important fact from the viewpoint of these notes is that in 1540 the new parish was given a special constitution by Act of Parliament. A Corporation of Wardens of St. Saviour's was set up, by which six wardens were to run the parish. The corporation still exists today, with an office over the gateway of the Borough Market. Most of the Tudor wardens in this corporation administered charities, as do their present successors.

The earliest volume of accounts in Southwark Local Studies Library is that for the parish of St. Olave in 1546-91 (see illustration). This period includes Mary Tudor's brief counter-Reformation and the subsequent Elizabethan settlement. Good runs of accounts over two centuries or more exist for the ancient parishes of St. George the Martyr, Southwark; St. Mary, Newington; St. Mary Magdalen, Bermondsey; and St. Mary, Rotherhithe. In addition to these general accounts, which became increasingly concerned with the Poor Law, there are major sets of accounts for specific church building campaigns: St. Olave's, 1737-40, when it was rebuilt by Henry Flitcroft; for St. Mary's, Rotherhithe, 1714-55, covering its rebuilding by John James and the subsequent payment of the debts; for the two churches of St. Peter, Walworth, and Holy Trinity, Newington, designed by Sir John Soane and Francis Bedford respectively; and finally, for St. Giles's Church, Camberwell, 1841-8 (by Sir Gilbert Scott), and for its daughter-

A list of surviving Southwark accounts can be found at the back of this book.

church of St. George, Camberwell, 1821-36 (by Francis Bedford). It should be noted that the dates of account books often go well beyond the years in which the church was actually built.

Queen Elizabeth I, 1566, and The Old Pretender, 1745

These churchwardens' accounts for St. Olave's in 1566 (right) include the entry 'P(ai)d the xxviii of June for a peell Ryngyng when the qwen went by........xii d'. St. Olave's Church stood immediately downstream of Old London Bridge on the Southwark side. Until 1750, the bridge was the only one in London and all travellers by land from the City and Westminster to the south therefore had to use it and to pass by the church, including Queen Elizabeth I on the occasion recorded here. It was for long a tradition to pay ringers to mark royal occasions such as the monarch's accession and birthday, and the anniversary of King Charles II's restoration. The ringers at Newington, however, inadvertently got into hot water in 1745, when they practised on June 10th, which happened to be the birthday of 'the Chevilear', or the Old Pretender, that is, James, the exiled son of King James VII and II. He was known as the 'Chevalier de St. George'. His father had been exiled in 1688, but the cause of his family - the Jacobite cause - was far from dead half a century later, for this was the year of the '45, the last Stuart attempt to evict the Hanoverians by force. It took a vestry meeting to rule that the ringers had acted 'not with any design to offend the Government...but that it was a Weekly Club Night with them'.

At A Meeting of the Parishioners in Vestry to Examine the reason of the Bells being Rung on the Tenth of June last, it Appeared to the Persons then Present that the Persons who then did Ring the Bells, did it not with any design to Offend the Government they Declareing they did not know it was the Pretenders Birth Day, but that it was A Weekly Club Night with them

Steph: Mott
Wm Wright
R. Withers
Wm Rutter
Zac Bourne
Rich Boulton
Edmond Cook

(marginal list of those present):
Mr. Mott
Mr. Wright
R: Boulton
R. Withers
Zac: Bourne
Wm. Cook
R: Griffin
Wm Rutter
Wm Skinner

Rotherhithe
Churchwarden's Accounts, 1709

This section is entitled 'The Acco(un)t of Mr. Elias Browne Principal Church Warden of the parish of St. Mary Rotherhithe in the County of Surrey for the Year 1709...'. The entries are all items of expenditure on poor relief. On the right-hand page, there is the entry, 'To the Widow Dobbins and her 3 children being sick and weak very poor and ready to perish.....................3 (shillings)' The next entry is 'To Eliz(abeth) Cutbert being sick and weak', but she was not ready to perish, and got only two shillings. A separate section of the book lists expenditure on the parish church. *(Right)*

Rates

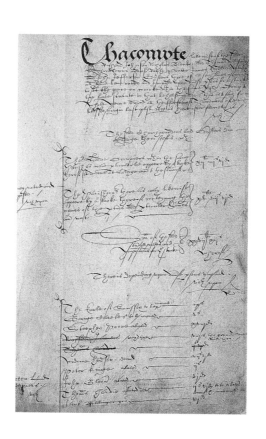

Compulsory rates for poor relief throughout England derived from the Elizabethan Poor Law of 1601, but assessments had been made on a looser basis in the 16th century. A list of contributors to the poor survives (left) among the churchwardens' accounts for St. Mary Magdalen's, Bermondsey, in 1599. It is headed by the Earl of Sussex, who owned Bermondsey House. The first proper series of rate books begins in 1635, in St. George the Martyr Parish. To begin with, assessments for a number of consecutive years were written in a single volume, and often they were placed in overseers' account books (or even in a 'pensioners' book' in the case of assessments for St. Giles's, Camberwell, in 1731-6). As the population increased, so the rate lists became longer, and they were then recorded in separate books. Subsequently, they were often divided geographically within a parish.

April **Rate, 182⅟** ——**EAST** **Division.**

No. of House.	No. of House.	Occupiers or Landlords compounding.	No. of Composition.	Receivers or Landlords not compounding, deemed Occupiers, and rated.	For Tenements as numbered, or now or late in the Possession of	When received.	Rental. £	Assessment. £ s.
13		High Street						
	147	John Harris		†			100	5 —
	148	John Hicks & Son		†			100	5 —
	150	Joseph Rutland					100	5 —
		for the Marshalsea		†				
	151	Thomas Fleming		†			48	2 8
		Elizabeth Smith		†			12	— 12
139	152	John & Cornelius Ruck		†			60	3 —
140	153	William Pugh		†			55	2 15
141	154	James Kirby Varden		†			42	2 2
142	155	William Kirkham		†			100	5 —
		William Kirkham		†			12	— 12
		Panger Court						
12		Daniel Redzwell		†			10	— 10
		William Saunders		†			10	— 10
		Occupier		†				

The Poor Law

Horselydown and Bermondsey introduced Landside and Waterside divisions, and St. George the Martyr used the cardinal directions. By the mid-19th century, both Bermondsey and Camberwell were using six divisions. Rate assessments do not survive for all the divisions in each possible year. The poor rate was the original compulsory rate, and then came the highway rate. In Georgian and Victorian times, there were church rates, churchyard rates, Navy and militia rates (during the Napoleonic Wars), sewer rates and main drainage rates. The various bodies of paving and 'improvement commissoners' between 1765 and 1855 made their own assessments, which are generally listed as paving rates. From 1856 onwards, various assessments were often put together as a consolidated rate or a vestry rate. The poor rate was the one which generally remained separate.

St. George's Rate Book, 1824

This shows a page from the poor rate book for the parish of St. George the Martyr for the April quarter of 1824 (left). The book starts with the East Division, which includes No. 150 Borough High Street, the premises of the Marshalsea Prison, whose Keeper or Deputy Marshal at that time was Joseph Rutland. One of his prisoners in April, 1824, was John Dickens, the father of the novelist, who had entered the gates as a debtor on the preceding February 20th, proclaiming as he did so that 'the sun had set upon him for ever'. John Dickens was in fact released after three months, but in 1842 the sun set upon the prison itself for ever. In 1870, Borough High Street was renumbered, and No. 150 became No. 211, which is the address of the Southwark Local Studies Library today.

Between late Elizabethan times and the very end of the Georgian period, each parish in Southwark generally had to devote more attention to the Poor Law than any other subject. The emphasis is clear in the churchwardens' and overseers' accounts for Rotherhithe, which were illustrated earlier. In two parishes, St. George the Martyr, Southwark, and St. Mary, Newington, the quantity of Poor Law records which survives is stupendous. Although the different runs of records certainly do not survive for all the possible years, there are more than enough examples to illustrate the normal workings of the local Poor Law, and to produce some unusual documents.

The overseers of the poor dispensed relief to their parishioners in the workhouse itself or in the form of outdoor relief. If they were doubtful whether a claimant for relief was a parishioner, the claimant would be taken before a magistrate to be questioned or *examined* about his antecedents, for relief was legally available in the parish where you had a *settlement,* that is, where you had been born or had been employed or had paid rates. Very many **settlement examinations** therefore exist, because many people came to London from the countryside, or drifted from one part of London to another. If the decision was that the claimant came from elsewhere, a **removal order** would be drawn up, but this could be postponed, as shown overleaf. Special **Scotch** and **Irish Passes** were used for cases from those countries.

In the cases of children in the workhouse, the parish sought to apprentice them out as soon as possible. A nine-year-old was sent off to a chimney sweep in one document illustrated here, and the parish in question also sent a seven-year-old to the same fate. Many Southwark children ended up in textile mills in the north of England. If the children were illegitimate, as was frequently the case, efforts were made to make the alleged fathers repay the parish for supporting their children. The various types of documents which resulted are discussed below.

The parochial Poor Law lasted generally in England until an Act of 1834 set up unions of parishes under new authorities called Boards of Guardians. In Southwark, however, several parishes were initially considered large enough to stand alone, and the real divide is not 1834 but 1869, when larger territorial units were finally set up. After that date, records are likely to be in the London Metropolitan Archives.

Settlement Examination: Handel, Musician

A claimant for poor relief in the parish of St. Mary, Newington, in 1796, one William Field, had little to say about his antecedents other than that he had been hired as a servant many years before by 'Frederic Handel of Brook Street in the parish of Saint George Hanover Square in the City and Liberty of Westminster in the County of Middlesex Musician'. Handel had died no fewer than thirty-seven years before William Field's settlement examination. His house in Brook Street (off Bond Street in the West End) still stands, and has recently been restored to be nearer its original appearance. *(Right)*

Workhouse minutes

A Workhouse Committee met weekly in St. George the Martyr Parish for many decades. Although it was ostensibly concerned with 'the house', its minutes in 1771 record a considerable attention to relief in the form of clothing: shirts, shifts and shoes are being awarded to numerous poor parishioners. In Georgian times, relief was often given in clothing rather than in money. As the 12-year-old Charles Dickens lived in the next street to St. George's Workhouse in 1824, it is sometimes claimed that the workhouse in *Oliver Twist* was modelled on it; and on the strength of that surmise, the copper from St. George's Workhouse has ended up in the Cuming Museum. *(Left)*

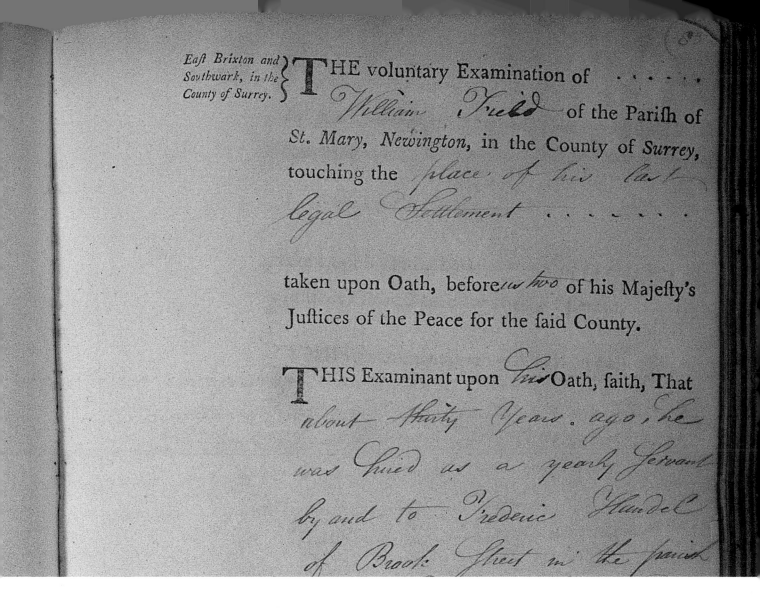

Mr. Pickwick in Southwark

In *Pickwick Papers,* Dickens placed the momentous meeting between Mr. Pickwick and Sam Weller at the White Hart Inn in Borough High Street, Southwark. What Dickens did not know is that the real Mr. Pickwick's father had had a connection with St. George the Martyr Parish just along Borough High Street to the south. The real Mr. Pickwick was the proprietor of the stage-coach which plied between London and Bath, as Dickens acknowledged in the novel, and in the document of 1799 shown here, his father's former servant, Luke Ashman, is claiming poor relief in St. George's Parish, eighteen years after he had been hired by Moses Pickwick at Witcomb near Bath in Somerset. Dickens himself was a parishioner of St. George's in 1824 and no doubt he would have been delighted to find out that the setting of his own personal and literary life had been linked with Moses Pickwick the elder. *(Left)*

Removal Order from Southwark

Elizabeth Jones claimed poor relief in St. George's Parish, but was considered by the overseers to be from elsewhere. She was questioned or examined before the local magistrates, who then issued this **removal order** in January, 1822. She was ordered to be removed to the parish of St. Paul, Covent Garden. *(Left)*

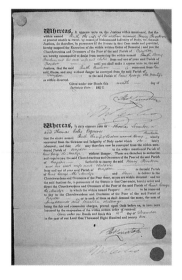

Removal from Croydon to Southwark

A document of 1822 orders that Henry Brookson and his family are to be removed from Croydon to the parish of St. George the Martyr, Southwark. Attached to it, however, are these documents to state, firstly, that Henry's wife, Ruth, is ill, and that the removal is to be delayed, and secondly, that she has happily recovered and that the original order is therefore confirmed.

It will be seen that St. George's is to pay £7 14s 0d to reimburse Croydon's expenses in the matter. *(Right)*

An Irish Pass

The archives of St. George the Martyr Parish include many Irish and Scotch Passes. Interestingly, the heading of the document shown here, an Irish Pass of 1820, invokes the City of London's jurisdiction in Southwark. The City arms and the Bridge House Estate's mark are shown side by side between the City's supporters. This is the nearest Southwark ever got to a municipal status before 1900, but it was as a subsidiary part of the City of London and not as an independent corporation. The two magistrates who have signed the document are City Aldermen. Mary Flinn, who is being returned to Ireland, is to be sent in the first instance to the parish of St. Magnus the Martyr, the first parish across the river in the City. Almost all Poor Law documents about settlements from Southwark's parishes emanated from courts where magistrates for the County of Surrey sat; this is therefore a relatively rare case of one surviving from the jurisdiction in Southwark of the City of London's magistrates. *(Right)*

Apprenticed to a chimney sweep

In Dickens's *Oliver Twist*, the elderly magistrate raises his quill pen to sign Oliver's indentures to apprentice him to a chimney sweep; he fails to find his inkwell, which is under his nose, but he does see that Oliver is horrified by his imminent fate. The magistrates decide to refuse the court's permission for the apprenticeship. In real life in 1820, Peter Simmons, a nine-year-old boy from St. George's parish in Southwark, was not so lucky, and was duly apprenticed to a chimney sweep at Hammersmith called James Brazier. Dickens would have liked the menacing hint of that surname. One of the magistrates who signed this indenture, David King, is the subject of another document in the library, in which he was appointed a Deputy Lieutenant of the County of Surrey.

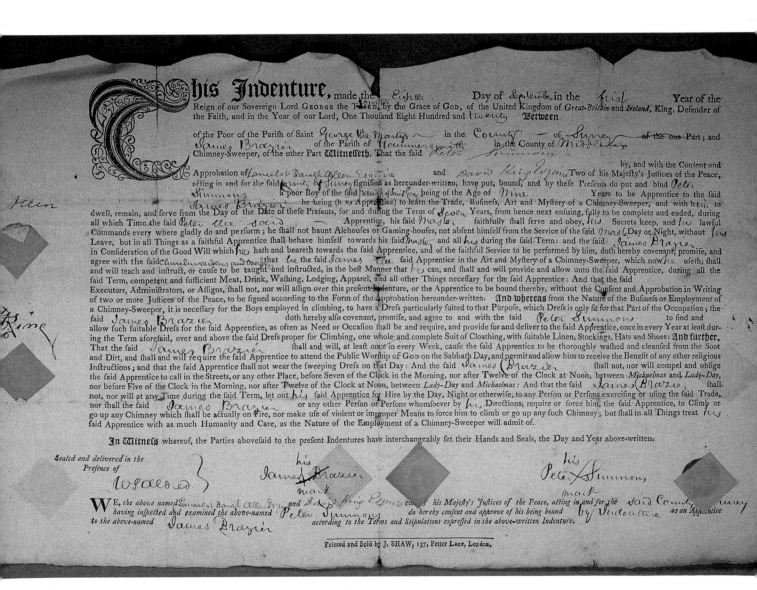

Sent to a cotton mill in Lancashire

A 13-year-old girl, Hannah Cornforth, was apprenticed to John Watson, a cotton manufacturer at Preston in Lancashire, in 1802. He was later bankrupted and children sent to him from Southwark were passed on to Messrs. Birch and Robinson, cotton manufacturers at Backbarrow in Lancashire. Northern mills frequently failed in this period, and pauper apprentices were liable to be passed from one mill to another. Some Southwark children were sent to the family firm of Sir Robert Peel, who later became Prime Minister. *(Top left)*

Bastardy Records

Claims for poor relief in a parish often came from women with illegitimate children, or who were about to give birth to such children. They were likely to be destitute. In such cases, the overseers of the poor would have the claimant questioned before a magistrate, in order to identify the father and to make him reimburse the parish's expenses. The first stage of the process was the issue of a **summons** to the alleged father, or a **warrant** for his arrest, either before birth or after birth. The court would then draw up an **adjudication in bastardy,** in which the crucial phrase was 'that the said Child hath been, and is likely to be further chargeable to the said Parish'. The magistrates would order that the father must repay the parish's expenses to date, and must subscribe a weekly sum to support the child. If the father ignored these orders, a further warrant would be issued, called a **warrant not obeying an order of filiation.** Such documents for St. George's Parish were issued at Union Hall, a magistrates' court built in 1782, which still stands in Union Street, Southwark, and is now in commercial use. *(Top centre)*

Two hundred parish children for disposal

One day around 1790 the postbag of the Vestry Clerk of St. George the Martyr included this 'short sketch of a plan of disposing of 200 parish children' by sending them to the mill of J. Bury & Co. at Hope Hill near Stockport in Cheshire. 'Parish children' was the label given to the unfortunates such as Oliver Twist, who had ended up in the parochial workhouse and who would be apprenticed out by the parish in due course. No children are known to have been sent to Cheshire as a result of this request, but many were sent to mills in Lancashire and Yorkshire and other northern counties (see above). *(Top right)*

Christ Church Workhouse

Christ Church Workhouse in Marlborough Street (later Gray Street), painted by G. Yates in 1826 (below right). Under the Poor Law Amendment Act of 1834, Christ Church Parish was put together with St. Saviour's Parish to form the St. Saviour's Union, which existed from 1836 to 1930. The institution pictured here existed well into the 20th century. Our view of workhouses is coloured by denunciations of the 'new Bastilles' of the 1834 Act, which were fully intended to be grim, to deter claims for poor relief. In practice, workhouses differed greatly over time. For much of their history, they had the roles of hostels for vagrants and the homeless, and what we would now call homes for old people.

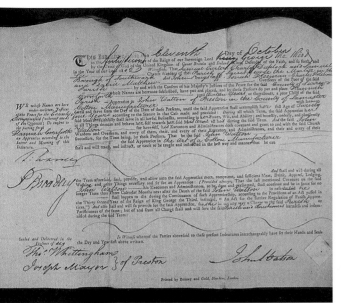

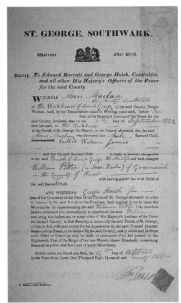

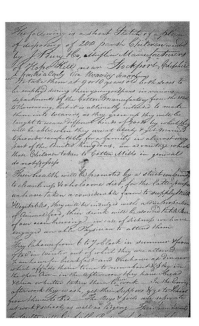

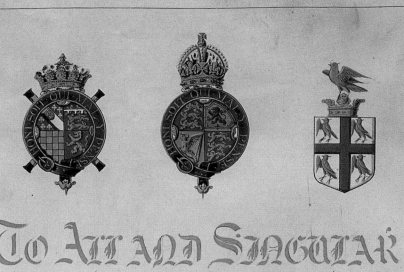

To All and Singular

to whom these Presents shall come Sir Albert William Woods, Knight Commander of the Most Honourable Order of the Bath, Knight Commander of the Most Distinguished Order of Saint Michael and Saint George, Garter Principal King of Arms, George Edward Cokayne, Esquire Clarenceux King of Arms and William Henry Weldon, Esquire, Norroy King of Arms, Send Greeting Whereas Frederick Redman Mayor of the Metropolitan Borough of Southwark, hath represented unto The Most Noble Henry Duke of Norfolk Earl Marshal and Hereditary Marshal of England, Knight of the Most Noble Order of the Garter, and one of His Majestys Most Honourable Privy Council, that by the Authority of the Act of Parliament 62 and 63 Victoria Cap 14 intituled "An Act to make better provision for the Government of London" Her late Majesty was pleased to enact with the advice and consent of the Lords Spiritual and Temporal and Commons in Parliament assembled, that the Area of Southwark should be a Borough. Also the

Council Records in the Twentieth Century

In contrast to the riches of the official archives from Georgian and Victorian times, the 20th-century material is relatively slight. The library holds all the Council and committee minute books from 1900 to 1965, but much of the rest is still in the Town Hall. Nevertheless, there is much of interest, especially as official photographs first feature in the archives after 1900. Photographs lend much life to any historical account, particularly one which deals largely with administration. Interest will often centre on individuals.

Grant of arms

The vestries down to 1900 did not bear heraldic arms, although they used badges to some extent in Victorian times. After 1900, however, the new Metropolitan Boroughs acquired arms as part and parcel of Edwardian civic pride. The illustration shows the upper part of the formal grant of arms to the Metropolitan Borough of Southwark in 1902, issued by the College of Arms in the City. The college is one of London's oldest institutions, and has an obvious and substantial interest in records in pursuing the work it undertakes. *(Left above)*

Freedom of the Borough

'The Freedom of the Borough' is a signal honour which has been granted since the Metropolitan Boroughs were formed in 1900. In the old mercantile boroughs of past centuries, such as the City of London, admission as a freeman was essential to the individual's exercise of a trade, and conferred important commercial and municipal privileges. In London's 20th-century boroughs, such rights have not applied, and instead the grant of the freedom by resolution of the borough council has been a public declaration of honour for any individual considered to have served the borough with conspicuous merit. In this case, Alderman William Brenchley was given the freedom of the Metropolitan Borough of Camberwell in 1932. He had served as Mayor of Camberwell in 1911-12 and he had served as a councillor at the borough's inauguration in 1900. Previously, he had served as a vestryman on Camberwell's St. Giles's Vestry. He was also honoured in the name of Brenchley Gardens at Honor Oak. *(Left below)*

Municipal ceremony in Tanner Street, 1929

Official photographers have always tended to follow the mayor to municipal events. In this case, at the opening of Tanner Street Recreation Ground in 1929, many important figures in Bermondsey at the time have been included. The tree is being planted by Dr. Alfred Salter, M.P. for Bermondsey, with the help of his wife, Ada; they were both central figures in the politics of Bermondsey between the wars. Ben Smith, M.P. for Rotherhithe, who later became a minister in Attlee's postwar government, stands to the right of Dr. Salter. Alderman Andrew Amos, Rector of Rotherhithe, stands behind Mrs. Salter. The mayor is Councillor G.A. Horwood; his son was to win the V.C. in the Second World War. The recreation ground had been the site of Bermondsey Workhouse. *(Right)*

Unofficial Records

Property Records

The term 'deed' usually refers to a document which gives the title to a property or a piece of real estate, but it may also refer to a personal legal document such as a will, an ecclesiastical licence or a certificate of holy orders. The major type of property deed to be found in the Southwark Local Studies Library is the lease. Almost all property was once held on lease, often for 99 years but sometimes for shorter or longer periods. A very long lease (500 or 1,000 years) was tantamount to a freehold. A 19th- or early 20th-century lease is usually quite easy to understand. A summary of its details will normally be written on the back or *dorse,* which to most people will seem to be the front. The vendor or *lessor* grants to the buyer or *lessee* a specified property - often shown in a small marginal plan - for a term of years beginning on a certain date (often one of the four quarter days: Lady Day or the Feast of the Annunciation (March 25th); St. John the Baptist's birthday or Midsummer Day (June 24th); Michaelmas Day (September 29th); and Christmas Day). A rent will be stipulated in most cases; there might be some restrictive covenants over the building's use; and the document will be signed and sealed by both parties or by just one of them (the lessor in the case of the lease proper, the lessee in the case of the counterpart or seller's copy of the lease). Leases may be sold or assigned; an assignment may be a separate document or it may be endorsed or written on the back of the original lease. Sometimes, an assignment required a licence from the original lessor. Under-leases may be granted, again subject in some cases to the lessor's agreement. In the case of a big estate, lease registers might survive, giving all the particulars of entire streets of properties. Such registers survive from the West Estate in Bermondsey. The heyday of the lease was before the First World War.

In the interwar years, many local businesses bought the freeholds of their premises, which had previously been leased from traditional landed estates. Courage's Brewery near Tower Bridge bought the freehold of its site from the Abdy Estate. Freehold housing first became a trend in the same period, but it was not until well after the Second World War that the old private estates of houses were widely broken up. In Southwark, this process typically took place in the 1960s. Such massive landholdings as the Rolls and West Estates were sold at that time. The one sizeable old landed estate to survive was Alleyn's Estate of God's Gift at Dulwich.

Mortgages and conveyances of freeholds also exist in some numbers after 1850. Public houses were invariably mortgaged, and mortgages are also found for business premises and even for non-Anglican churches (see illustration, top right). Today, we associate the mortgage with a private house or flat, but in the days when most houses in Southwark were leased or rented, the mortgage of a house was uncommon. Prior to the sale of a property, printed particulars would often be issued. They also count as deeds and might give as much useful information as an actual sale. The printed particulars of a large Victorian estate, which will generally have a map attached, are invaluable for the history of a district.

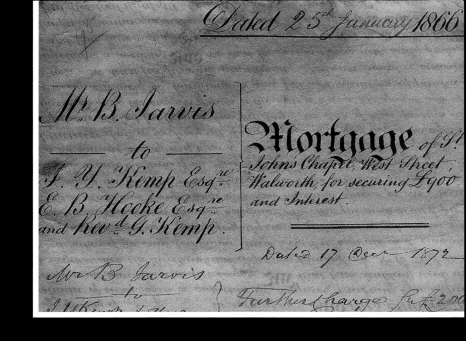

The library's earliest deed

The oldest document in the library comes from the records of St. Olave's and St. Saviour's Grammar School Foundation. It is dated May 17th, 1347, and records a gift by William Amyel, a miller, and Agnes, his wife, to Richard Paterlying. The property in question was on Bankside in St. Margaret's Parish (a mediaeval parish which was later incorporated in St. Saviour's). It had on its west and south sides property in the ownership of Lord Miles de Stapleton, who was one of the original Knights of the Garter in 1348.

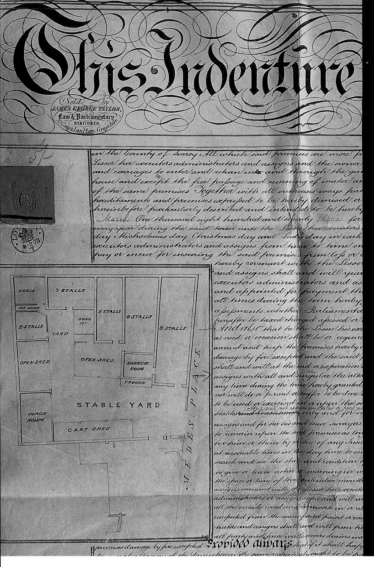

A Victorian lease

This counterpart lease of February 3rd, 1873, illustrates the type discussed overleaf. It is a lease of stables and other buildings at the rear of the Artichoke Tavern in Newington Causeway, near the Elephant and Castle, for 49 years from March 15th, 1873, at the cost of £100 a year. As was usual by the Victorian period, the deed bears a marginal plan (which is highly useful to local historians in itself) and is written on a sheet of vellum with a printed heading, which was sold by a law stationer. This document is also an example of an indenture or an agreement between two or more parties; a party might be one person, or several. Anciently, two copies of such a document would be cut so that the indented or wavy edges could always fit together in the case of a dispute, but by 1873 such edges had long been a matter of form. 'Indentures' often referred in the 19th century to the documents by which apprenticeships were formally agreed.

Above: Goldsworthy Terrace, Lower Road, 1803, on Sir William Gomm's estate.

Field Marshal Sir William Gomm

Field-Marshal Sir William Maynard Gomm was the owner of a large estate at Rotherhithe between 1822 and 1875. He had been gazetted an ensign (that is, awarded a commission of the lowest rank) in the 9th Regiment at the early age of ten, in 1794 (on account of the death of his father on active service in the West Indies), and saw active service from 1799 onwards. Afterwards, he served under Wellington in the Peninsular War. In later years, he acted as a garrison commander in Jamaica, Mauritius and India. From Jamaica in 1840 he sent a turtle to his old chief, the Duke of Wellington, and this letter (above, left) thanks Gomm for the gift. At that time, Gomm was a Major-General and held the K.C.B., which had been conferred on him in 1814. He ended his days as a Field-Marshal, as Colonel of the Coldstream Guards and as Constable of the Tower of London.

Friern Manor Farm

The change from open countryside
to the bricks and mortar of a Victorian
suburb came no swifter than in East
Dulwich. The huge block of land between
East Dulwich Road, Peckham Rye, Wood
Vale and Lordship Lane was almost entirely
undeveloped at the beginning of the 1860s.
Within 25 years it was a fully-fledged new
suburb. Most of that land had belonged
to Friern Manor Dairy Farm, and it had
been a stable agricultural estate for
centuries. In 1865 it was going to be sold
for development, and an abstract of title was
drawn up on the owner's behalf. It runs to
many dozens of pages and includes the fine
map illustrated here. Each field on the farm
is named in the accompanying schedule.
It seems strange to think of field names in
built-up areas of Southwark today, but they
were once common even in Bermondsey.

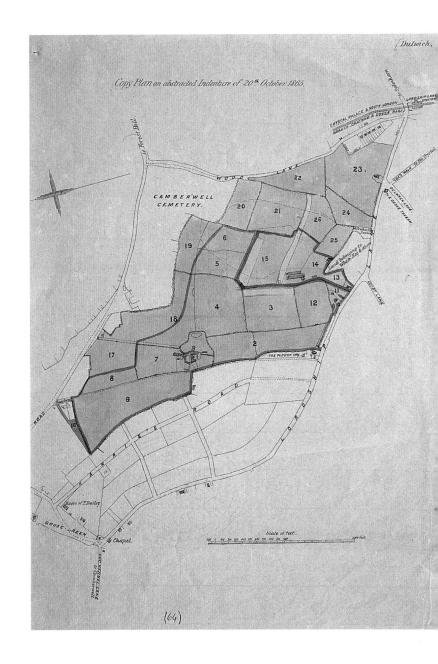

A manorial court at the Elephant and Castle

Manorial records might form a distinct category in many record offices, but Southwark Local Studies Library holds a few oddments only, and as they are all tied to the management of estates, they might reasonably be represented under property records.

The Elephant and Castle Public House, which gave its name to the important junction at whose centre it stood for so long, first appears by name on March 21st, 1765, in a volume which records the meetings of the Court Leet of the Manor of Walworth. A manor has many definitions, but in the 18th century it referred chiefly to a *jurisdiction*, which might or might not be connected to a landed estate. In the case of Walworth, the lord of the manor was an ecclesiastical body, the Dean and Chapter of Canterbury Cathedral, and there was certainly a sizeable estate to administer in 1765. The Elephant and Castle Public House had previously been a farrier's called the White Horse; the change probably occurred in about 1760, after New Kent Road had been built to take traffic from the Old Kent Road towards the new Westminster Bridge. The Court Leet concerned itself largely with ditches, fences and pavements.

Personal Papers

Personal papers typically encompass diaries, letters, account books, wills and records of births, marriages and deaths. The diaries held in Southwark Local Studies Library are not of much moment, but they are still local period-pieces, chiefly Victorian. One interesting collection consists of various papers from a well-to-do young resident of Champion Hill in Camberwell in early Victorian times, Samuel Edwards, plus a daguerreotype portrait of him in 1846 (when he was 18), which is the earliest original photograph held in the library. (The first photograph taken in London is only seven years older.) The papers include his honeymoon diary (in 1854), which records his travels on the Continent, and an account book, in which there are innumerable daily entries for 'punch and lunch'. He paid 6d. (2 1/2p) to go 'to town'. Clearly, he lived on a level well beyond that of the vast majority of Southwark's population in the mid-1800s. The daguerreotype portrait is remarkably well preserved.

Victorian memorial cards

James Stevens Curl wrote a book in 1972 entitled *The Victorian Celebration of Death*. One small aspect of the subject was the issue of memorial cards. Of the two illustrated here, one is in remembrance of John Day, Vestry Clerk of St. George the Martyr Parish, Southwark, who died in 1863. He was a successor of Archibald Campbell Russell (see page 7). The other commemorates an heroic figure in the history of Victorian London: James Braidwood, Superintendent of the London Fire Brigade, who was killed in the Great Fire of Tooley Street in 1861. The fire was said to have been the biggest since the Great Fire of 1666, and Braidwood's funeral procession to Abney Park Cemetery at Stoke Newington was certainly one of the largest seen in the 19th century. Personal records relating to death might seem very minor, but to family and local historians they are important sources of information.

Wills

The vast majority of wills held in the Southwark Local Studies Library are probate copies, prepared when the wills were proved (that is, accepted as genuine by an official body). Before 1858, this was done in a church court. The local court was that of the Archdeaconry of Surrey, but *all* the wills held in Southwark were proved in the Prerogative Court of Canterbury, the principal or provincial church court. The probate certificate in this case relates to Catherine Everitt of Back Street, Horselydown, who died in 1826, and it bears the signature of a proctor at Doctors' Commons, which was the college of church lawyers sited near St. Paul's in the City. Dickens's character and *alter ego,* David Copperfield, began to train as a proctor in the novel.

Letter to Camberwell, 1731

Thomas Bruce, Earl of Ailesbury, sent this letter from Brussels to his niece, Henrietta Ogle, at Camberwell Vicarage in 1731. Although just a few years before, Daniel Defoe had written in amazement at London's growth in his great work, *A Tour Through the Whole Island of Great Britain,* the city was not to engulf Camberwell for a few more decades. Camberwell remained a country village, albeit populated by a sprinkling of rich Londoners. So it was sufficient for Lord Ailesbury to address his letter airily 'at Camberwell in Surrey near London'. No doubt Madam Henrietta Ogle was relatively well-known, as she was related to the Vicar of St. Giles's. Lord Ailesbury had become a Roman Catholic and a Jacobite in the late 1600s and lived overseas.

Records of churches

The Southwark Local Studies Library is not a diocesan record office, and so original Anglican church registers are not deposited in it. Some other types of ecclesiastical parish records, however, have been inherited with what are meant to be civil parish records. In addition, the deposit of records from Southwark Cathedral has brought material from parishes which have merged with it. Personal papers from priests are always liable to turn up, for they went into descendants' or solicitors' hands. The records of private estates are likely to include counterpart deeds of dealings with parishes over land, especially in the 19th century, when new churches, mission halls, schools and parsonages were built in great numbers. The counterparts, which were kept by the estates, will record conveyances of land for all these purposes.

The Southwark Local Studies Library is an official place of deposit for Methodist records, and that status has brought about a large collection of minute books, account books and registers going back to the early 19th century. Other denominations are represented quite randomly. A few Baptist records have been preserved, including a photograph album from the family of Charles Haddon Spurgeon, 'the prince of preachers' (above), who founded the Metropolitan Tabernacle at the Elephant and Castle. That great Baptist church still flourishes, but most of Southwark's formerly numerous Baptist churches are no more.

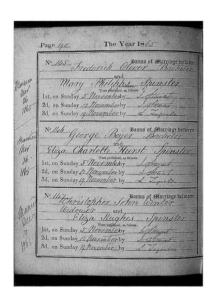

Banns of Marriage

Although Anglican parish records are now deposited in the London Metropolitan Archives, the library has inherited a few items from the 19th century. There is a run of banns' books for St. Mary Magdalen's Parish, Bermondsey, in which the three readings of banns of marriage are recorded, and also (in the margin) there are notes about the actual marriages.

A Wesleyan Methodist Register

The first Methodist church in Southwark was set up by John Wesley himself in 1743 in a building in Snowsfields which had been erected for another denomination. By the mid-19th century, Methodist churches were numerous in the area. The building in Deverell Street (see illustration) belonged to the mainstream Wesleyan Methodists (for by Victorian times the original Methodists had split into several separate groups). This baptismal register from 1849 uses the printed pages which were first introduced for Anglican churches under Rose's Act in 1812.

Candidates Names	Parents Names	Occupation	Residence	Age	No. of Chil[d]n	Time of OHS
Matthew Gadd	Margaret	Widow	York St	8	4	4
Matthias Field	Matthias & Eliza	Boatbuilder	Roth. Wall	8	4	4
Richard Trott	Rich.d & Mary	Waterman	Bond St	8	3	4
William Lacey	Martin & Mary	Deal Porter	Ram Alley	8	.	3
Will.m J. Pocock	Will.m & Eliz.th	Bricklayer	Brickfield	8	3	3
Samuel Cooke	Samuel & Ann	Laborer	Bell Alley	8	3	2
Will.m J. Dally	James & Lydia	Policeman	Adam St	8	3	2
Will.m Spencer	John & Martha	Laborer	Oak Place	8	4	2
George Austin	John & Mary Ann	Boatbuilder	Adam St	10	6	1

The charity school in Rotherhithe in 1826 (right), and a list of prospective pupils in 1836 (left).

School Records

Local state schools were first set up by the London School Board, which began its work under an Act of 1870. The schools passed into the hands of the London County Council in 1904 and then to the Inner London Education Authority in 1965. Not until 1990 did the borough council run local schools. So the Southwark Local Studies Library has no records from state schools; they are held by the London Metropolitan Archives, and to some extent by the schools themselves. What the library does hold are records from church and charity schools. A great many papers are held concerning the St. Mary

Newington Schools at the Elephant and Castle in the 19th and early 20th centuries, partly because of the Cumings' collection and partly through the agency of George Waine, who ran a family furnishing business in Newington Butts. Another considerable batch of material relates to the charity school in Rotherhithe. A series of minute books of its governing body is held in the library, from which an illustration is shown here. Prospective pupils are regularly listed, with the names, addresses and occupations of their parents. Mr. Peter Shilham has calendared the entire series from 1778 to 1869.

Records of prisons

Southwark had five prisons subsequent to the Middle Ages: the King's Bench, the Marshalsea, the White Lion or Surrey County, the Clink, and the Borough Compter. The last of these attached to the City's jurisdiction in Southwark and was closed when that jurisdiction was allowed to lapse. The Clink, although notorious, was originally no more than a manorial lock-up for the Bishop of Winchester's estate. The remaining three were much larger. The White Lion was the county prison for Surrey and survived in Horsemonger Lane (the present Harper Road) until the 1870s. The King's Bench and the Marshalsea were two of the principal debtors' prisons of London (the third being the Fleet across the river). Their records are chiefly to be found in the Public Record Office, but their sites and their control were at least partly private matters, giving rise to property deeds and personal papers. Two such items are illustrated here. Although they do not form a distinct category in archival terms, they are of local importance and merit special attention.

A Half-Share in the Marshalsea's site

The Marshalsea Prison stood at least in part on private land. In 1774 a half-share in that land was owned by Lady Caroline Leigh, sister of the Duke of Chandos. In this deed, which is just one stray part of a transaction, she is transferring the property in trust. *(Top right)*

An appointment to the Marshalsea in 1689

The Marshalsea Prison had two sites in Southwark. On its second site, where Southwark Local Studies Library now stands at 211 Borough High Street, it lasted for just 31 years, but because John Dickens was a prisoner in that period, it has achieved lasting notoriety. The earlier site, however, which was only a few yards farther north, where Mermaid Court now runs, lasted for up to four and a half centuries. It was in that long phase that its story was particularly grim, for the prisoners were not Dickensian debtors but religious and political captives (in Tudor and Stuart times) or ordinary criminals. One of its more notorious keepers was Christopher Lowman, who is mentioned with loathing in pamphlets of the early 18th century. The document illustrated here is his appointment in 1689 as Deputy Marshal and Keeper of the prison under the hand and seal of Sir Edward Villiers, Knight Marshal, who was a kinsman of the 17th-century Dukes of Buckingham. As it is a document issued by a Crown official, it is written in Latin, for Latin was used for formal state documents until as late as 1733. This is one of the few documents held in Southwark which dates from the time of 'William and Mary' (King William III and Queen Mary II), the joint sovereigns who followed the deposed King James after the 'Glorious Revolution'. *(Below right)*

Dated 8th June 1774

Lady Caroline Leigh
to
The Duke of Chandos
and an.²

Lease for a Year.

611

23039

Omnibz Christi fidelibz ad quos presens scriptum pervenit Edward Lillies mil Marescall Hospitij dni Regis Edne Regine salutem in dno sempiterno Sciat me prefat Edward Lillies integritat directioni et probe circumspectioni Christopheri Gorman plurimum confidens et dictis bonis causis considerationibz me ad hoc specialiter moventibz concessisse et confirmasse et per presentes concedere confirmare prefat Christophero Gorman officium submarescalli hospitij dni Regis et dne Regine Palatij sui Westmr et custod prison suis una cum officio deputate Marescall et Marescalt hospitij dni Regis et dne Regine unacum omnibz feodis regarde pfituis avantag et emolumentquibzcunq eisdem officijs seu cuicouq alti spectud seu aliquo modo pertinen Et per presentes Gorman submarescallu dni prefat et custod prison dni prefat et submarescalt marescalt hospitij prefat nominare ordinare constituere et admittere per presentes Habend tenend et gaudend dict officia submarescalt dne dni Regis dne Regine Palatij sui Westmr prefat custod prison prefat ac submarescalt marescalt prefat eid Christophero Gorman durante vita sua naturali se bene gesserit cum omnibz prefat feod vadijs regard officius avantag et emolument quibzcunq que ut eisdem officijs seu cuicouq alteri ad aliquod tempus antehac legitime pertinet sive datus fuerunt qui eisdem officijs seu cuicouq alti de jure spectant et pertinent In cuius rei testimonium sigillum meum presentibz apposui dat scriptu... die Augusti Anno dni 1689 Annoque Regni Regis et Regine Anne...

Edward   William

Military and Wartime Records

Local volunteer units were founded during the French Revolutionary and Napoleonic Wars when the threat of invasion was at its height, in 1798 and again in 1803. Each parish had its own unit. The Southwark Local Studies Library holds records only of St. Mary, Newington's unit, because Richard Cuming was a member of it and, being a Cuming, kept all the papers relating to his service. These Napoleonic volunteers were stood down when the threat of invasion receded. Similar units re-emerged in 1859 and 1860 when it was thought (more improbably) that the Emperor Napoleon III might order an invasion. Tennyson stirred the nation into action with his poem, *Riflemen, form!,* and the Prime Minister, the ever-belligerent Viscount Palmerston, built fortifications along the coast. Corps of Surrey Rifle Volunteers were formed in Camberwell, Walworth and Bermondsey. The one in Camberwell was to be known for over a century as the First Surrey Rifles. Bermondsey's and Walworth's units were re-designated in 1882 as the 3rd and 4th Volunteer Battalions of the Royal West Surrey Regiment, which was widely known as 'The Queen's'. In 1908, the names were changed to the 22nd and 24th Battalions of the London Regiment. The Southwark Local Studies Library holds the papers of the 24th Battalion from Walworth, which Major J.M.A. Tamplin TD did so much to gather together and which greatly informed his substantial work, *The Lambeth and Southwark Volunteers* (1965). The direct succession of Volunteer or Territorial units in Walworth ran from 1860 to 1967, and for most of that period the depot was in New Street (later renamed Braganza Street after Queen Catherine of Braganza, the wife of King Charles II, to whom 'The Queen's' alluded). Most of the papers from Braganza Street naturally refer to the two world wars, but there are many from the Victorian years of the Volunteers, and from the later peacetime periods of the unit's existence.

Victorious entry into Lille, 1918

The 1/24th Battalion of the London Regiment formed part of the 47th (London) Division on the Western Front during the First World War. Towards the end of the war, the division liberated Lille in northern France as the Kaiser's army was rapidly pushed back. The Band and Drums of the battalion from Walworth, headed by Drum-Major W. Mew, led the division in a ceremonial entry into Lille on October 28th, 1918. This remarkable photograph therefore captures a significant moment in military history, in which soldiers from Southwark took part (right below). A poster hurriedly printed in Lille to welcome the division as the city was liberated, is preserved in the Local Studies Library.

Sketches from wartime Egypt

While the 1/24th Battalion of the London Regiment was campaigning on the Western Front, the 2/24th Battalion was stationed at Salonika and in Egypt. The Turks of the old Ottoman Empire were their adversaries in the Levant. One member of the battalion, H. Page, drew numerous sketches during his service in Egypt, which ranked at that time as a British Protectorate. The failure of the campaign at Gallipoli is often recalled, but it is too often forgotten that General Allenby led British forces to victory in the Middle East in 1917-18, including the capture of Jerusalem. These sketches of military life in that theatre over eighty years ago seem much more remote than mementoes of service in France, yet Egypt had British military garrisons for over seventy years until as recently as the 1950s. *(Right)*

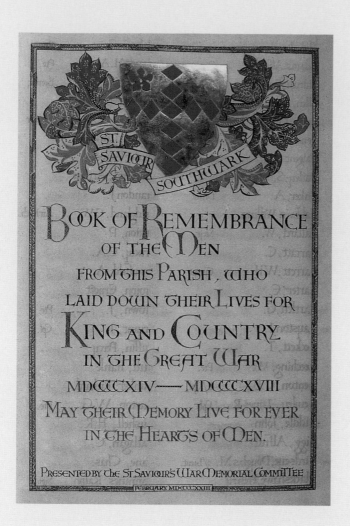

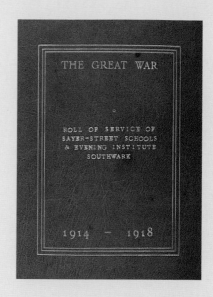

A school roll of Service

Rolls of service were made for the London County Council's schools after the First World War. This one comes from Sayer Street, off the New Kent Road near the Elephant and Castle. Huge numbers of men served in the armed forces in 1914-18, and such lists can be of great value to family historians.

St. Saviour's Roll of Honour

The First World War gave rise to many substantial memorials in the principal streets and squares all over England. Less well-known are the numerous rolls of honour and rolls of service which also resulted. In the case of St. Saviour's Parish in Southwark, the memorial in Borough High Street was accompanied by a book of remembrance prepared on behalf of the St. Saviour's War Memorial Committee in February, 1923. It is the most elaborately illustrated manuscript in the library's collection.

Evacuees from the Blitz

Many children were evacuated from Southwark in the Second World War, especially during the Blitz of 1940-1. Evacuation was arranged through schools, which were largely run by the London County Council. Official records have therefore ended up in the London Metropolitan Archives. The Southwark Local Studies Library has unofficial memorabilia only, such as the batch of letters, of which this is one, which came from a Miss Wiles, a former Sunday school teacher in Camberwell, whose pupils ended up in Devon and Berkshire. The countryside was a strange place to many poor children from prewar London, who had never had the chance to travel far from home.

Records of Businesses

Too many works of local history have followed the traditional model of 'church and manor'. The world of commerce and industry is foreign to them. In the London Borough of Southwark, such an approach would be ludicrously inadequate, for industry was the linchpin of much of its life. Old Southwark and Bermondsey in particular were major manufacturing and commercial districts until well after the Second World War. The handling of cargoes at the riverside wharves and in the Surrey Docks formed the backbone of their commercial life. Foodstuffs were among the principal cargoes, especially in Bermondsey. Peek, Frean's for biscuits; Crosse and Blackwell's for tinned foods; Shuttleworth's for chocolates; Pearce, Duff's for custard powder and blancmange; and Hartley's for jam were all prominent local businesses. The Southwark Local Studies Library does not hold records of these big companies (see the next section), but it does keep an interesting collection of records from smaller businesses, including those of a well-known 19th-century shipbreaker; various hop merchants from in and around the Borough High Street; Jones & Higgins, Peckham's former department store; and numerous small manufacturers.

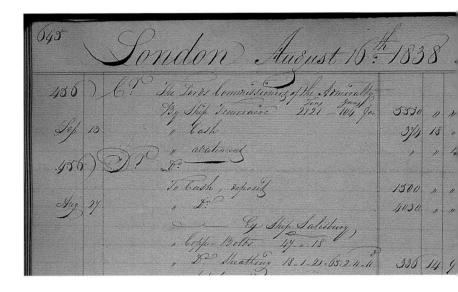

The Fighting Temeraire

The Southwark Local Studies Library holds the ledger from John Beatson's shipbreaking business at Rotherhithe from 1835 to 1858. One entry in 1838 records the sale to Beatson by the Lords Commissioners of the Admiralty of a very famous ship, the *Temeraire*, which had been one of the principal ships of the line at the Battle of Trafalgar in 1805. Under the command of Captain Eliab Harvey, it had a position astern of the *Victory* itself as Nelson's fleet bore down on its adversaries. Harvey was one of only three individuals mentioned in the vote of thanks concerning the battle which was agreed by the House of Commons in January, 1806, the others being Nelson himself and his deputy, Collingwood. J.M.W. Turner set the seal on the ship's reputation by his painting (now in the National Gallery), which is widely known as *The Fighting Temeraire*. For Turner, the ship was a symbol of the 'wooden walls of England' of his youth, when they saved England from invasion by Napoleon. The painting was the centrepiece of an exhibition at the National Gallery in 1995, with the corollary that Southwark's ledger had its finest hour as an unlikely exhibit in Trafalgar Square.

The first railway ticket

Southwark was the terminus of London's first railway, the London and Greenwich Railway, which was opened on December 14th, 1836. It was a very substantial business undertaking. The ticket shown here is therefore one of the first railway tickets issued in London. The line traversed the eastern part of the old town of Southwark and the whole of Bermondsey and Rotherhithe on a considerable viaduct, which must have seemed a stupendous work when it was new, for much of it stood away from buildings. The station at Spa Road, which lasted until 1915, had served as a temporary terminus for a few months in 1836, before London Bridge Station was completed. Strangely, a railway hotel - the Bridge House Hotel - had been built to George Allen's design two years ahead of the station, and so Southwark had the distinction of having London's first railway hotel before it had London's first railway station.

Records elsewhere

The archives held in the Southwark Local Studies Library are very considerable, but it must never be forgotten that many important sources for Southwark's history are kept elsewhere. The London Metropolitan Archives is mentioned many times in this book, for it holds Anglican parish registers, records of the local boards of guardians and surviving records of state schools, to take just three categories of obvious significance. The borough to the west of Southwark, the London Borough of Lambeth, has an Archives Department which collected records from south London long before other boroughs decided to do so. Many manorial records from Southwark are held there, and innumerable property deeds. The Corporation of London Records Office represents the government of the City of London, and as that government once encompassed the old town of Southwark, many details of Southwark's history may be researched in that repository. Southwark also fell into the County of Surrey, and so the Surrey History Centre at Woking holds much material of local interest. Those great national collections, the Public Record Office and the British Library, naturally hold countless documents of local pertinence. This collection of illustrations of documents ends with one from the library of the Society of Antiquaries of London, which happens to be the earliest document to mention any part of the London Borough of Southwark by name.

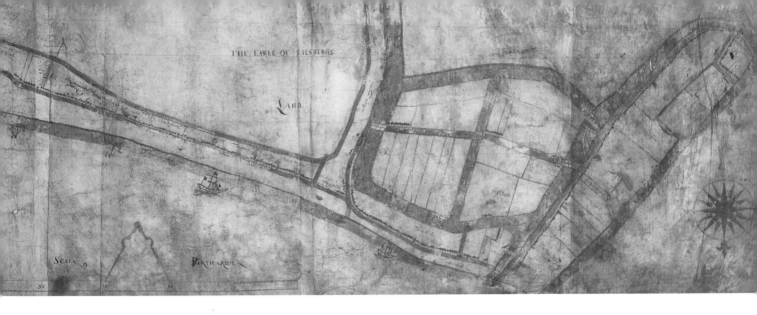

The earliest map of Jacob's Island

The London Borough of Lambeth Archives Department holds in its collection a map of Bermondsey which dates from about 1610. The map shows the area which was later to be known as Jacob's Island, just to the east of St. Saviour's Dock. The context of this map is apparently the acquisition of a large estate in Bermondsey by Robert Cecil, first Earl of Salisbury, a couple of years earlier. It shows a considerable degree of development along the riverfront even at that stage.

(Reproduced by kind permission of the London Borough of Lambeth Archives Department.)

Biscuits in Bermondsey

Peek, Frean's was one of Southwark's biggest businesses. It was founded in Mill Street, Bermondsey, in 1857, and later moved to Drummond Road, near the London and Greenwich railway line, where it operated until the 1980s. Its records are now deposited in Reading University Library, as a result of a connection with Huntley & Palmer's of Reading.

Pope Constantine's Charter to Bermondsey

The earliest document which relates to Southwark is an 8th-century papal charter, whose text is preserved in a 12th-century register from Peterborough Abbey in the collection of the Society of Antiquaries of London. Peterborough Abbey was a very important monastery in the Kingdom of Mercia in the Midlands, which became the mother-house of numerous monasteries in other parts of England where Mercian power afterwards obtained. London and the south-east of England came under Mercian rule in the later 7th century, and it must have been then that a monastery was first founded in Bermondsey. By the early 8th century, Mercian power had temporarily ebbed, and that of Wessex had emerged. The Abbot of Bermondsey no doubt considered that a degree of protection from higher ecclesiastical authority would be wise in a situation in which different kings and bishops successively held sway around him. The result was a charter from Pope Constantine I (who held office from 708 to 715), in which the rights of the abbot and the local bishop are carefully defined. The abbot's name is Hedda and the place-name is given as *Vermundesei*, meaning 'the island of Beornmund'. So Bermondsey appears in a written record just over a century earlier than Southwark itself. The abbey to which the charter refers almost certainly disappeared in the Viking invasions of the 9th century. The familiar Bermondsey Abbey of the later Middle Ages was a separate foundation in the Cluniac Order at the end of the 11th century.

(Reproduced by kind permission of the Society of Antiquaries of London.)

Tanpits at Bevingtons' works. 1931

There's nothing like leather

Leather tanning was a prominent local industry for some centuries. Substantial firms had premises in Bermondsey until well after 1945. Bevingtons & Sons was a leading firm in the trade, occupying a large site in Abbey Street and further property in St. Thomas Street. The firm moved to Leicestershire in the 1980s. Its records are now kept in the London Metropolitan Archives.

Maritime Southwark

This photograph of the Thames at Rotherhithe in 1914 emphasizes how busy the river was in those days. Barge-building and barge-repairing were undertaken locally. The Surrey Docks took in cargoes from Canada and Scandinavia, chiefly in timber and foodstuffs, and the biggest dock in the system, the Greenland Dock, could handle 14,000-ton Cunarders. In this view, colliers are seen near the jetty of the South Metropolitan Gas Works. Gas records are now to be found at Partington in Manchester, for all the local manufacturing works have long since closed. The Surrey Docks were run from 1909 by the Port of London Authority, whose records have ended up in the Museum in Docklands at Poplar.

Vestry Minutes in the Southwark Local Studies Library listed by Parish

St. Olave, *Southwark, 1552-1900 (7 volumes) (Mediaeval parish)*

St. John, *Southwark (also called St. John, Horselydown), 1879-1900 (2 volumes) (The parish was a subdivision of St. Olave's in 1733)*

St. Saviour, *Southwark, 1854-1900 (10 volumes) (The parish was formed in 1540 by the merger of the mediaeval parishes of St. Margaret, Southwark, and St. Mary Magdalen Overy; it was the most important parish in Southwark, whose church became Southwark Cathedral in 1905; the London Metropolitan Archives holds the minutes from 1557 to 1854)*

St. Thomas, *Southwark, 1836-1899 (2 volumes) (The parish of the precinct of St. Thomas's Hospital, amounting to only eight acres; the hospital was founded in the early 13th century but the parish was not certainly designated until the late 15th century; the civil parish was merged with that of St. Olave, 1896; the ecclesiastical parish was merged with that of St. Saviour, 1898; the church served as the chapter house of Southwark Cathedral until 1988)*

Christ Church *(usually called Christ Church, Surrey), 1863-1900 (3 volumes) (Founded in 1671 by the subdivision of St. Saviour's Parish; the London Metropolitan Archives holds the minutes from 1756 to 1863)*

St. George the Martyr, *Southwark, 1716-1900 (19 volumes) (Mediaeval parish)*

St. Mary Magdalen, Bermondsey, *1674-1900 (50 volumes) (Mediaeval parish)*

St. Mary Rotherhithe, *1673-1900 (45 volumes) (Mediaeval parish)*

St. Mary, Newington, *1583-1900 (23 volumes) (Mediaeval parish, mentioned in Domesday Book as Walworth)*

St. Giles, *Camberwell, 1674-1900 (52 volumes) (Mediaeval parish, mentioned in Domesday Book)*

NOTES:

The first and last dates are given of a run, but there are often gaps. The first five parishes above were not designated vestries under the Act of 1855, but they continued for ecclesiastical purposes. The rest were designated under the Act.

Four new districts, which were created in the 1820s within the ancient parishes, were treated as civil parishes to some extent, but did not have vestry minutes of their own:

St. George's, Camberwell (formed from St. Giles's, Camberwell)
St. Peter's, Walworth (from St. Mary's, Newington)
Holy Trinity, Newington (from St. Mary's, Newington)
St. James's, Bermondsey (from St. Mary Magdalen's, Bermondsey)

Surviving Churchwardens' Accounts

St. Margaret, *Southwark, 1444-1540 (in the London Metropolitan Archives)*

St. Olave, *Southwark, 1546-91 (1 volume), plus the journal of rebuilding the church, 1737-40*

St. Mary Magdalen, *Bermondsey, 1599-1794 (6 volumes)*

St. George the Martyr, *Southwark, 1609-1860 (5 volumes and loose papers)*

St. Mary, Newington. *1632-1847 (4 volumes), plus accounts of the building of St. Peter's, Walworth, and Holy Trinity, Newington, 1821-31*

St. Mary, Rotherhithe, *1707-1890 (5 volumes), plus accounts of the trustees for rebuilding the parish church, 1714-1755*

St. John, *Southwark (St. John, Horselydown), 1740-1 and 1751-2 (loose accounts only)*

St. Giles, *Camberwell: the ledger of the church building committee, 1841-8 (1 volume) and the ledger and other records of the New Church Committee (for St. George's, Camberwell), 1821-1836 (3 volumes)*

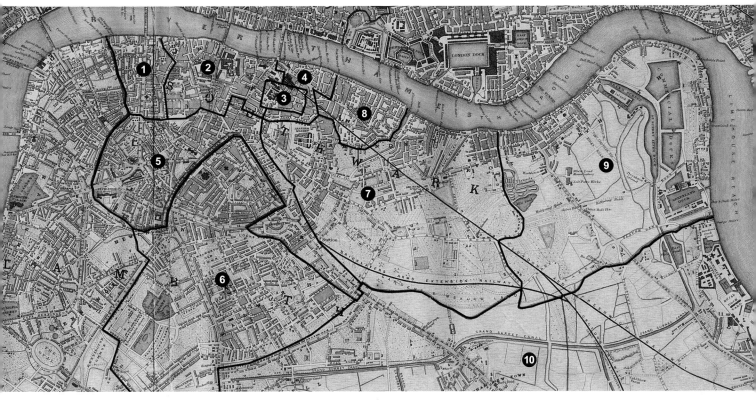

The northern part of Southwark from a map of 1846 published by B.R. Davies. The ancient parish boundaries have been indicated:

1. Christ Church
2. St Saviour
3. St Thomas
4. St Olave
5. St George the Martyr
6. St Mary, Newington
7. St Mary Magdalen, Bermondsey
8. St John, Southwark
9. St Mary, Rotherhithe
10. St Giles, Camberwell

The descent of the borough council from local mediaeval parishes.

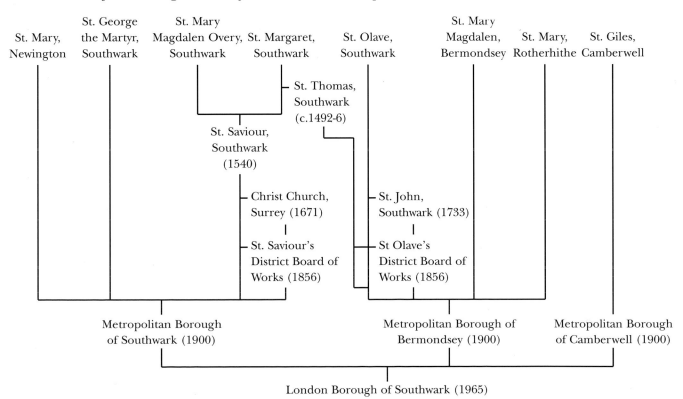

Index and useful addresses

Useful addresses

Southwark Local Studies Library
211 Borough High Street, London,
SE1 1JA (020 7403 3507)
Monday and Thursday, 9.30-8.00; Tuesday
and Friday, 9.30-5.00; Saturday, 9.30-1.00

London Metropolitan Archives
40 Northampton Road, London, EC1R OHB
(020 7332 3820)

Lambeth Archives Department
52 Knatchbull Road, London, SE5 9QY
020 7926 6076)

Corporation of London Records Office
P.O. Box 270, Guildhall, London, EC2P 2EJ
(020 732 1251)

Surrey History Centre
130 Goldsworth Road, Woking,
Surrey, GU21 1ND (01483-594594)

Public Record Office
Ruskin Avenue, Kew, Richmond,
Surrey, TW9 4DU (020 8876 3444)